WHIRLERS AND TWIRLERS
SCIENCE FUN WITH SPINNING

VICKI COBB
ILLUSTRATED BY STEVE HAEFELE

THE MILLBROOK PRESS
BROOKFIELD, CONNECTICUT

Published by The Millbrook Press, Inc.
2 Old New Milford Road
Brookfield, CT 06804
www.millbrookpress.com

Library of Congress Cataloging-in-Publication Data
Cobb, Vicki.
Whirlers and twirlers : science fun with spinning / Vicky Cobb ; illustrated by Steve Haefele.
p. cm.
Includes index.
ISBN 0-7613-1573-X (lib. bdg.)
1. Rotational motion—Juvenile literature. [1. Motion—Experiments. 2. Experiments.]
I. Haefele, Steve, ill. II. Title.
QC133.5 .C63 2001
531'.113—dc21 00-055433

1 SIMPLY SPINNING

BET YOU CAN'T DO A FEW SPINS AND THEN WALK A STRAIGHT LINE. EASY, YOU SAY. AFTER ALL, SKATERS CAN SPIN LIKE TOPS AND SKATE AFTERWARD. BUT SPINNING IS THE NUMBER-ONE DIZZINESS PRODUCER OF ALL TIME.

Get a baseball bat or a yardstick or some other waist-high stick. Put the end of the bat on the ground and hold the handle upright. Put your forehead on the end of the handle and walk around the bat three times. Stand up and see the world turn! Now try to walk a straight line. You are definitely not designed to be a spinning object!

Believe it or not, your ears keep you well balanced. Even stranger, they use sloshing liquid to do it. Here's how: Each of your ears has a place deep inside your head called the inner ear. The inner ear has three pretzellike tubes arranged at right angles to each other.

To get an idea of this three-dimensional arrangement, point your index finger as if you're saying "bad dog!"; stick up your thumb; and straighten out your middle finger so it points toward your other hand.

Every time your head moves suddenly, the liquid in these tubes also moves. This motion is detected by tiny nerves that tell you how to adjust your body to keep your balance. But when there's too much sloshing, the body can't adjust quickly enough and you get dizzy.

semicircular canals

INNER EAR

cochlea

Even if you're not designed to be a spinning object, there are plenty of things that are. How many can you name? Here's a list to get you started: wheels, fans, eggbeaters, the Earth and other planets, helicopter rotors . . .

COOKING
with
IGOR

You can make things spin. All you need are two forces moving in opposite directions.

To spin a coin, hold it on its edge by resting one finger on top of the coin. As you take your finger off the top edge, flick the side of the coin with the index or middle finger of your other hand.

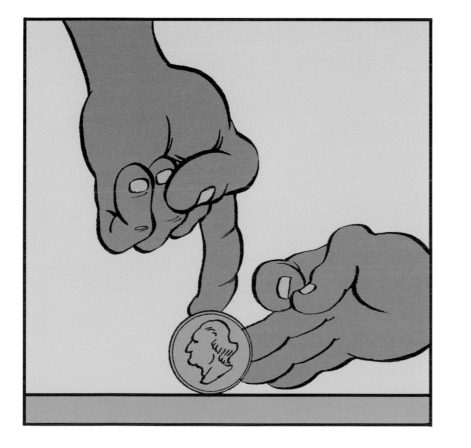

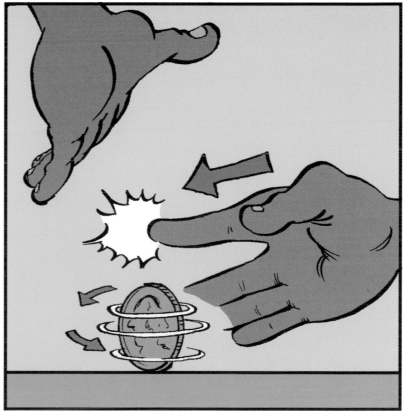

The top of a plastic film can is a great spinner. Press the inside of the cap so it curves slightly outward. Put it upside down on a table and place your index fingers on either side of the cap. To spin the cap, flick one finger forward and one back at the same time. Experiment by putting small circles of paper colored with markers inside the caps. Here are some designs you can try. The colors will blend as they spin. Blink your eyes a few times as you look at a spinning color wheel. Your blink seems to stop the action!

LET'S WALK THROUGH THE HOUSE AND SEE HOW MANY THINGS WE CAN SPIN WITHOUT BREAKING THEM.

Try bottles, pens, paper clips, or your TV remote. See if you can tell the difference between a hard-boiled egg and a raw egg by the way they spin. When you spin oddly shaped objects, they find weird points to spin on. Try spinning a funnel.

If you think you've been successful with things that are not designed to spin, wait until you start playing with some champion whirlers and twirlers.

2  A WHIRL ON A STRING

Ever see a cowboy rope a steer? He whirls the lasso over his head. Then, at just the right moment, he lets go with the hand that's doing the whirling. The lasso sails through the air and loops over the steer's head. The cowboy pulls, and the lasso closes around the animal's neck. He's caught!

The cowboy may not know it, but he uses some laws of nature to lasso that steer. These laws apply to all objects that move rapidly in circles, even you.

IT'S HARD TO UNDERSTAND HOW FORCES AFFECT SPINNING THINGS. SO IT'S VERY IMPORTANT TO DO THE ACTIVITIES IN THIS BOOK. PUT YOURSELF IN ACTION AND MAKE DISCOVERIES.

A button whirler shows some of the amazing actions of spinning objects. You will need a large button (about an inch in diameter) and some very strong thread such as fishing line, dental floss, or heavy-duty nylon. Cut a piece of thread that is about 3 feet long. Pass the thread through the two holes in the button. If the button has four holes, thread the two that are diagonally across from each other. Bring the ends of the thread together and knot them.

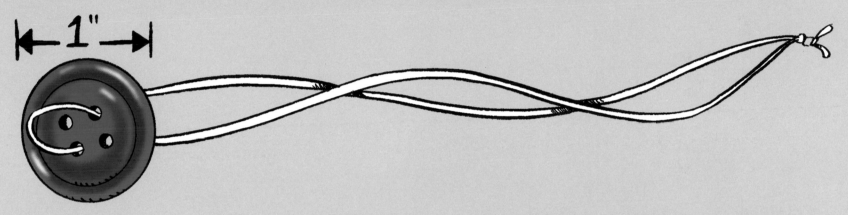

Experiment with your button whirler as if it were a lasso. Do this outside in a large space so that no one gets hit by a flying button. As you twirl the button over your head, it will travel in a circle in the air as if there were no gravity.

There are two forces acting on the whirling button. The combination produces its circular path. One force, called *centripetal force*, is the pull of the thread on the button toward the axis of the circle.

AH, THE LANGUAGE OF SCIENCE. DON'T LET IT SCARE YOU. SCIENTISTS MAKE UP WORDS TO DESCRIBE WHAT THEY SEE. WHEN YOU KNOW THE WORDS, IT'S EASY TO UNDERSTAND WHAT THEY'RE TALKING ABOUT.

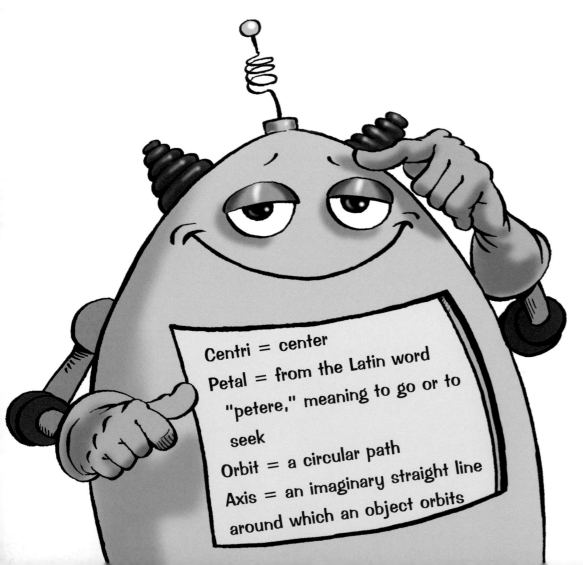

Centri = center

Petal = from the Latin word "petere," meaning to go or to seek

Orbit = a circular path

Axis = an imaginary straight line around which an object orbits

The center of the circular path made by a whirling object is its axis. Your hand is the axis of the whirling button.

The second force is the speed you give the button when you whirl it. This force pulls the button away from the axis. It acts in the opposite direction from centripetal force. The faster the button moves, the greater the force away from the center. Since the button can't fly away as long as you hold the thread, its path is the result of these two opposite forces—a circular orbit.

SUN

MOON

HOUSTON, NOT ENOUGH SUN BLOCK!

"EARTH

THE EARTH IS WHIRLING LIKE THE BUTTON. THE SUN IS ITS AXIS. INSTEAD OF A STRING, THE INVISIBLE FORCE OF GRAVITY PULLS THE EARTH TOWARD THE SUN. BUT ITS SPEED KEEPS IT IN A CIRCULAR ORBIT THAT TAKES ONE YEAR TO COMPLETE.

THE MOON REVOLVES AROUND THE EARTH. GRAVITY BETWEEN THE EARTH AND MOON HOLDS THE MOON IN ITS ORBIT.

V.C.

Give your whirling button a good spin and let go. It will fly farther than you could have thrown it. The only problem is that it's hard to control its direction. The released button travels in a straight path, but its direction depends on where it is in its orbit at the moment you release it. Have a whirling button-aiming contest with a friend.

THERE ARE TWO OLYMPIC EVENTS THAT RELEASE WEIGHTS FROM A SPIN — THE HAMMER THROW AND THE DISCUS.

JUST BE SURE TO LET GO!

You can make your button whirl faster without adding force directly to it. Can you guess how? Pass the knotted end of the thread of your button whirler through the hole in the center of a spool of thread. Hold the spool with one hand and the thread with the other. Start the button whirling by rotating the spool. The button will swing out from the spool as it begins traveling in a circle. When the button is whirling nicely, pull on the thread. As you shorten the length of thread between the button and the spool, what happens to the motion of the button?

When you pull the thread, you make the distance between the button and the axis—the spool—shorter. The closer the button is to the axis, the faster it will spin.

RIGHT HAND WHIRLING BUTTON

LEFT HAND PULLING STRING

THE SPEED OF THE EARTH IN ITS ORBIT IS 66,641 MILES PER HOUR, OR ABOUT 19 MILES EACH SECOND. THE EARTH IS THE THIRD PLANET FROM THE SUN. MERCURY IS THE PLANET THAT IS CLOSEST TO THE SUN. IT IS ALSO THE SPEEDIEST, MOVING AT 107,132 MILES PER HOUR, OR ALMOST 30 MILES A SECOND.

PLUTO, ONE OF THE FARTHEST PLANETS FROM THE SUN, IS ONE OF THE SLOWEST. IT ORBITS AT 10,604 MILES PER HOUR, OR ABOUT 3 MILES PER SECOND.

When an ice skater spins, she knows this law of nature: When she draws her arms close to her body she twirls faster. The closer her arms are to the axis of spin, the faster she twirls.

PULL IN YOUR ARMS AND LEGS, IGOR.

WHEN YOU PULL IN YOUR ARMS AND LEGS, YOU MAKE THE MATTER OF YOUR BODY CLOSER TO THE AXIS OF YOUR SPIN, SO YOU SPIN FASTER.

When a cowboy twirls a lasso, his hand becomes the axis. The spinning force acts on the weight of the rope, making the loop open. If the cowboy didn't twirl the rope, the loop wouldn't open and he couldn't slip it over the steer's head.

Here's another experiment for your button whirler. You can turn it into a spinning whistler. The thread through the center of the button will be its axis. Slip your index fingers through the loop at each end of the thread. Slide the button to the center. Make little circles with your hands so that the button starts moving in a circle. This winds up the thread on each side of the button. Gently move your hands away from each other. Then bring your hands together. By moving your hands apart and together, you make the button spin first one way then the other. It winds up the thread in one direction and unwinds it in the other direction. The button spins so quickly that you can't see it change direction. There is also an instant when the loop is completely unwound. You have to pull very slowly to see these things. To make it easier to see what's happening, put a spot on the button with a magic marker. The spot disappears when the button is spinning, but it briefly appears in the moment when the button changes direction.

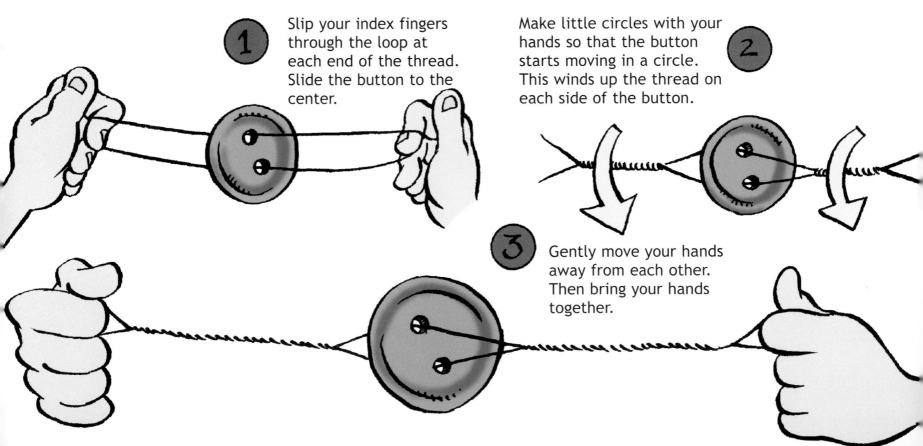

1 Slip your index fingers through the loop at each end of the thread. Slide the button to the center.

2 Make little circles with your hands so that the button starts moving in a circle. This winds up the thread on each side of the button.

3 Gently move your hands away from each other. Then bring your hands together.

As the button builds up speed, it sets the air around it in motion. You hear this moving air as a whistle.

SOME BUTTONS MAY BE BETTER WHISTLERS THAN OTHERS. TRY A REALLY BIG BUTTON. WHAT HAPPENS WHEN YOU LET GO OF ONE END? WHAT HAPPENS WHEN YOU TOUCH THE EDGE OF THE SPINNING BUTTON TO A TABLE OR A GLASS? LISTEN FOR A NOISE THAT WILL DRIVE YOUR PARENTS NUTS! EXPERIMENT AND FIND OUT.

3  WIND WHIRLERS

Isn't it amazing that the world keeps revolving around the sun without ever slowing down? Here on Earth, it seems that everything you start spinning needs a force to keep it spinning. That's because there is a force here that's always slowing things down. It's called *friction*. When two surfaces move against each other there is friction. Even moving against air creates a kind of friction. But in space there is no friction, so the Earth keeps moving at the same speed forever.

In the old days, people used the force of falling water to overcome friction and keep waterwheels turning. Waterwheels turned millstones to grind grain into flour.

Steamboats used the force of steam to turn paddles that churn the water, to move the boat forward.

What do you need to produce a force? Some kind of energy.

Falling water, steam, and electricity are sources of energy that keep things moving. Can you name some others?

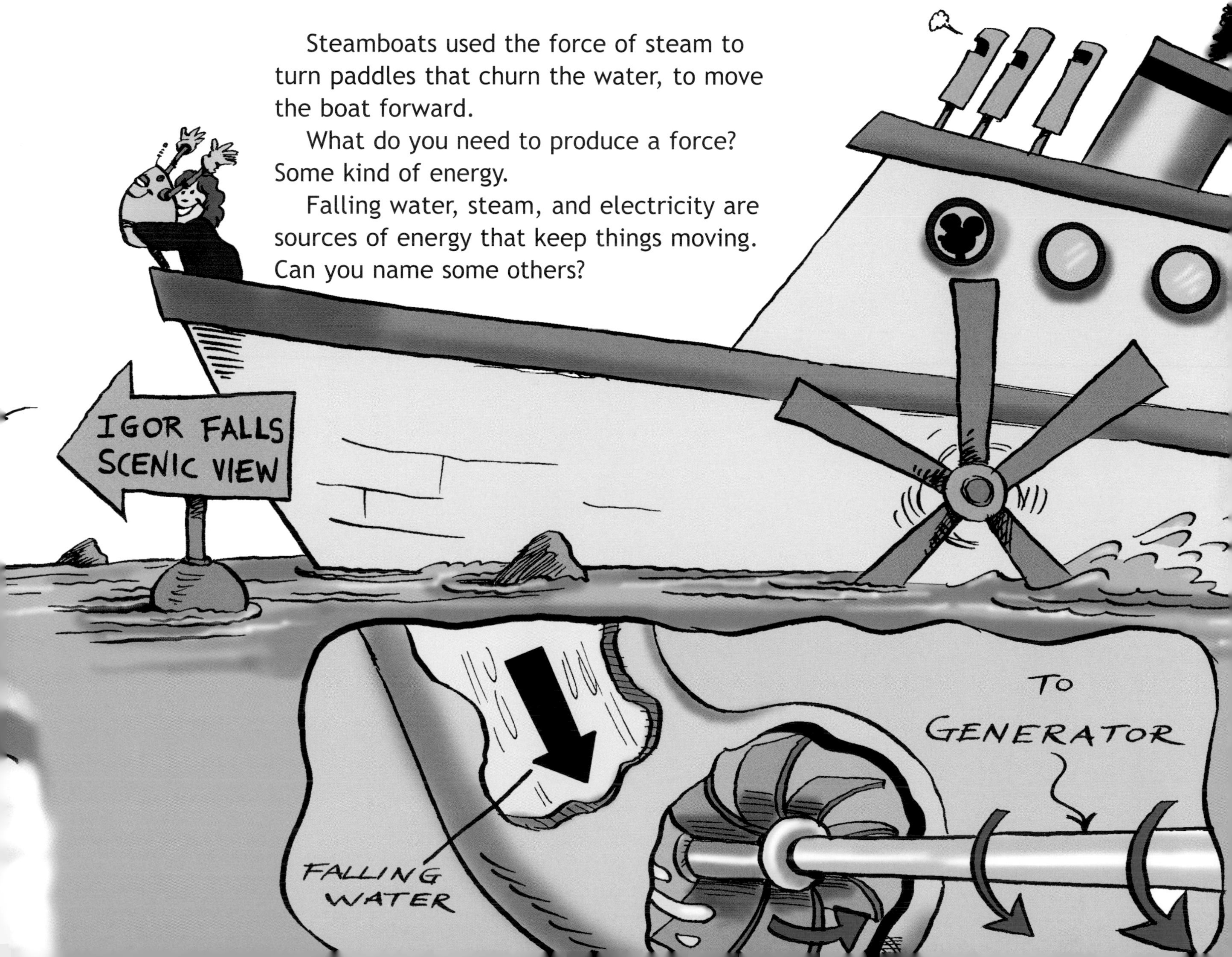

IGOR FALLS SCENIC VIEW

FALLING WATER

TO GENERATOR

One source of energy that is always available is wind. A sail catches the wind so a boat can move. A pinwheel is four sails around a central axis. Here's how to make a pinwheel.

You will need:

4"
4"
4"
4"

a 4-inch square of construction or heavy gift-wrap paper

a plastic straw

scissors

a straight pin

cellophane tape

① Fold the paper in half on the diagonal.

② Open the paper and fold it on the other diagonal.

③ Cut about 2 1/2 inches along each diagonal fold from the corner toward the center.

④ Fasten the tip of one of the split corners in the center of the paper with a small piece of tape.

⑤ Going clockwise, skip the next corner and fasten the tip of the next corner in the center with another piece of tape.

⑥ Continue around the pinwheel, skipping a tip and fastening a tip.

⑦ Snip off a piece of straw that is 1/2 inch long.

⑧ Stick a pin through the center of your pinwheel. Pass it through the 1/2-inch length of straw and insert it through the remaining length of straw about 1/2 inch down from the end.

① ② ③ $2\frac{1}{2}"$ ④

⑤ ⑥ ⑦ $\frac{1}{2}"$ ⑧

Turn the pinwheel to make sure it spins freely.

Experiment blowing on your pinwheel. Discover which direction you need to blow in order to produce a spin. Can you make your pinwheel spin by walking with it? What happens when you take it outside?

WINDMILLS ARE GIANT PINWHEELS. SINCE WIND IS CLEAN ENERGY, ENGINEERS ARE LOOKING INTO USING WIND TO GENERATE ELECTRICITY. WIND POWER STATIONS NEED A LOT OF LAND IN A PLACE WHERE THE WIND IS STEADY.

What happens if you turn a wind spinner so that it's spinning horizontally to the Earth? The person who first thought of trying this invented the idea of the helicopter. Actually, you can find this design in nature. The maple seed spins through the air like a small helicopter. You can see how by making a maple-seed toy.

1. Cut two 1-inch-wide strips along the long side of a regular sheet of paper.

2. Lay one strip on top of the other and twist the two strips together, leaving about a third untwisted.

3. Separate the untwisted strips and fold them so they form a V-shaped propeller.

4. Stand on a chair, hold the model maple-seed with the twisted part hanging down, and drop it.

IT SAYS "CHAIR!"

1"

HOW ABOUT HAVING A FALLING CONTEST, IGOR? WHICH FALLS FASTER, A MAPLE-SEED SPINNER OR A BALL THE SAME WEIGHT? EXPERIMENT AND FIND OUT. TAKE TWO NEW STRIPS OF PAPER AND CRUMPLE THEM INTO A SMALL BALL. IT'S THE SAME WEIGHT AS OUR MAPLE-SEED SPINNER. DROP THE MAPLE-SEED SPINNER AND THE CRUMPLED PAPER BALL AT THE SAME TIME. WHICH DROPS FASTER? HOW DOES THE DESIGN OF THE REAL MAPLE SEED HELP SPREAD ITS SEEDS?

A spinning propeller stirs the air so that the pressure on top of the propeller is less than the pressure underneath, and the device goes up. A whirligig is a toy that works like a helicopter.

A whirligig is fun to make, but it takes a bit of practice to get good at launching it.

You will need:

a milk carton

scissors

white household glue

a bamboo skewer for shish kebob about 8 inches long

① Cut the propeller from the carton so it matches the size and shape shown in Step 1.

② Punch a small hole in the exact center of the propeller.

③ Holding the propeller at each end, twist it in opposite directions. This gives it a three-dimensional shape that can catch the air.

④ Cut the sharp tip off the bamboo skewer. Insert one end through the hole in the propeller. Put glue around the hole on both sides of the propeller. Make sure the skewer is at right angles to the propeller. Let the glue dry for at least three hours.

Now for the challenge. To launch your whirligig, you have to spin the skewer. Put the center of the skewer vertically against the heel of your left hand. Hold it in place with the fingers of your right hand. Slide your right hand forward as you bring your left hand back. The twirling whirligig takes off and rises spinning in the air until it falls to the ground. If it happens to go down instead of up, reverse the direction of your hands.

If your whirligig doesn't fly very well, it may need more weight at the ends of the propeller. You can add a gob of glue, or two or three staples, to each end.

A WHIRLIGIG IS LIKE AN UNCONTROLLED HELICOPTER WITHOUT STEADY POWER. A HELICOPTER DOESN'T FLY VERY FAST. BUT IT CAN TAKE OFF AND LAND VERTICALLY. SO IT'S VERY USEFUL FOR GETTING PEOPLE OUT OF TIGHT SPOTS.

4  YO-YOS

A yo-yo is a double wheel with a string attached to its axle. What happens when you let it dangle on the end of its string? Nothing very exciting. All it does is rotate as it untwists its string. But its behavior becomes completely different when you know how to use it.

Wind the string around the axle until you reach the loop at the end. Slip your middle finger through the loop so that it is between the first and second knuckle. Then throw the yo-yo to the ground.

1. MAKE SURE THAT THE YO-YO STRING IS THE RIGHT LENGTH FOR YOU. THE STRING SHOULD BE THE DISTANCE FROM THE GROUND TO YOUR WAIST.

2. TO THROW THE YO-YO PROPERLY, BEND YOUR ELBOW AND COCK YOUR WRIST TOWARD YOURSELF.

Where's my waist?

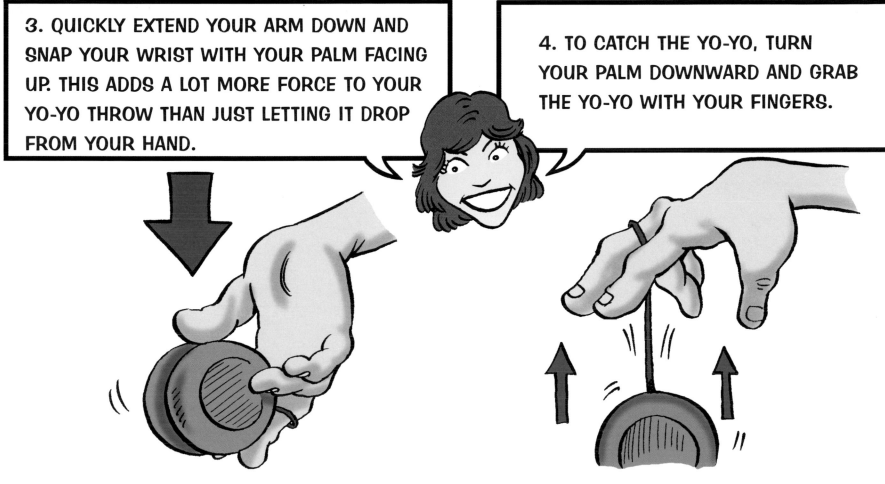

3. QUICKLY EXTEND YOUR ARM DOWN AND SNAP YOUR WRIST WITH YOUR PALM FACING UP. THIS ADDS A LOT MORE FORCE TO YOUR YO-YO THROW THAN JUST LETTING IT DROP FROM YOUR HAND.

4. TO CATCH THE YO-YO, TURN YOUR PALM DOWNWARD AND GRAB THE YO-YO WITH YOUR FINGERS.

The yo-yo spins down the string until it is completely unwound. Give the yo-yo a gentle tug when it reaches the end of its string. The yo-yo spins *up* the string, defying gravity, returning to your hand.

Here's something not many people notice when they use a yo-yo. If you watch carefully, you will see the string on one side of the axle going down and on the opposite side coming up. It is as if the string jumped across the axle at the moment it reached the bottom. To see what really happens, unwind your yo-yo. As you near the end of the string, keep turning the yo-yo as you unwind the string. Watch what happens to the string on the axle as you reach the end. Keep turning to see the mystery!

When you drop a yo-yo, the unwinding string forces the yo-yo to spin as it falls. The wheels of the yo-yo store the energy of the spin so that it will keep on spinning after it reaches the end of the string. Wheels that keep on spinning long after the force that started them spinning is gone are called *flywheels*.

A POTTER KICKS A HEAVY FLY-WHEEL TO TURN A PLATFORM THAT LETS HIM SHAPE HIS POTS. THE ENERGY FROM A KICK TO THE FLYWHEEL SPINS THE PLATFORM FOR MANY TURNS. A YO-YO IS A KIND OF FLYWHEEL.

The axle of the yo-yo passes through a loop at the end of the string. In a normal throw, friction between the axle and the string grabs the axle of the spinning yo-yo. Since the yo-yo keeps spinning, the only place it can go is back up the string.

If you don't tug at the yo-yo when it reaches the bottom, the yo-yo will remain there spinning, or "sleeping," in the loop. If you don't let it sleep too long, a tug will return the yo-yo to your hand.

ZZZZZZz

HOW TO PUT A YO-YO TO SLEEP:

1. MAKE SURE THE STRING IS NOT TOO TWISTED.
2. THE HARDER YOU THROW THE YO-YO, THE FASTER IT SPINS AND THE BETTER IT SLEEPS.
3. TRY FOR A TWO-TO-FOUR-SECOND SLEEP TO START. PRACTICE. THE WORLD RECORD SLEEP IS TWENTY-FIVE SECONDS.

After you've been yo-yoing for a while, you'll notice that the string is twisted. If you let the yo-yo dangle on the end of the string, it will rotate as the string untwists itself. But no matter how twisted the string gets, a properly thrown yo-yo never untwists when it is spinning up or down the string. It stays spinning in the direction it starts spinning. Check this out for yourself.

At first, this looks like it's no big deal. But wait. It's the reason you can ride a bicycle. When bicycle wheels are not turning, the bicycle falls over. But when you pedal, you can easily stay balanced. In fact, the faster you go, the easier it is to balance. There is a name for this: the *gyroscope effect*. You'll learn more about amazing gyroscopes later.

SWOOOOSH!

PLOP!

5  TOPS

When does a top flop? A top flops when it stops, of course. A spinning top has the amazing ability to balance itself on a point—something totally impossible when it is not spinning.

WAYS TO SPIN TOPS

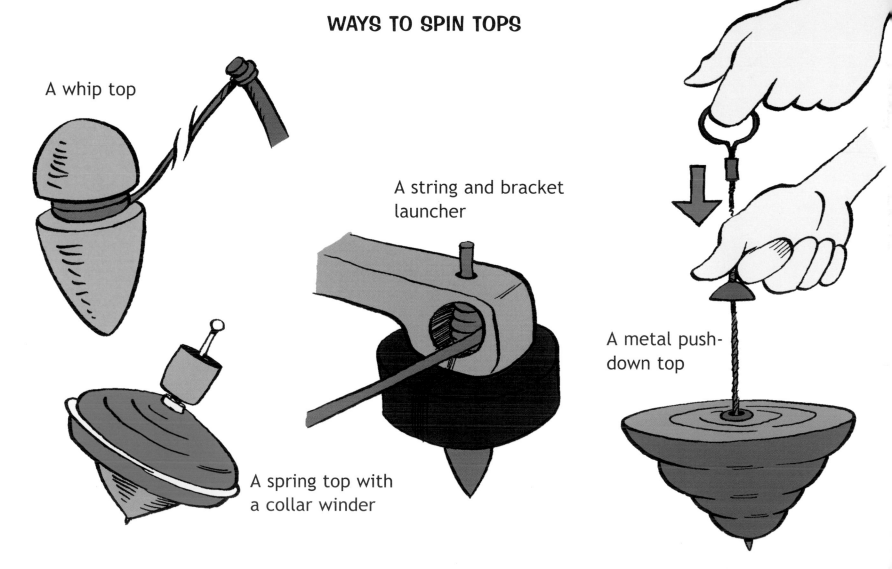

A whip top

A string and bracket launcher

A metal push-down top

A spring top with a collar winder

Experiment with spinning tops. You can use a top from a toy store or you can make your own. Here's a top that's easy to make. You need a large button and two twist ties. Insert a twist tie through a hole in the button. If the button has two holes, insert the second twist tie. If the button has four holes, the twist ties should be diagonally across from each other. The button should be slightly closer to one end of the twist ties than the other. Twist the twist ties together on both sides of the button. The longer end will be the end you spin. The shorter end will be the axis point.

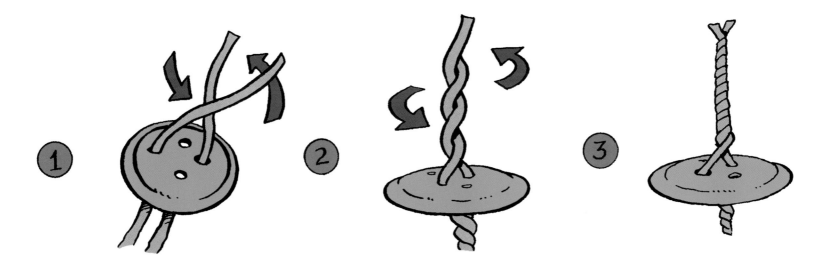

Rest the spinning point of your top on a level, open surface. Hold the end of the twist ties with your thumb and index finger, and quickly move your thumb forward as you move your index finger back. It takes a little practice to give your top a nice long spin. This is a pinch spin top.

All tops spin the same. When the top is perfectly vertical, it spins around its axis without tilting. This kind of spinning is called "sleeping." When it sleeps, the top resists any change in the direction of its spinning axis. But sooner or later a battle between forces starts. Friction between the tip of the top and the ground slows it down. Gravity now acts on the top and it starts to topple. But it is still spinning fast enough to resist toppling. So as soon as it starts to fall over, it rights itself. The result is that the top of the axis moves in a circle. This has the fancy name of precession. As the top slows down, the precession gets larger and larger, until gravity finally wins. What is the direction of precession? Is it in the same direction as the spin of the top? When a top is sleeping, there is no precession.

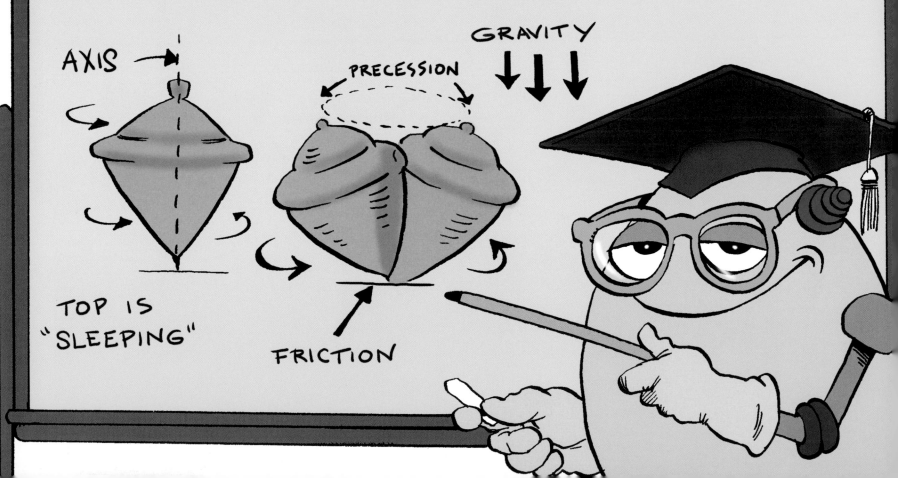

AXIS

TOP IS "SLEEPING"

PRECESSION

GRAVITY

FRICTION

The Earth is like a giant top spinning on its axis. This motion creates night and day. The Earth also has precession. It wobbles very slowly on its axis, making a complete circle every 26,000 years.

Here are some top-notch experiments for tops: If possible, use a top from a toy store that is designed to spin steadily for a long time.

1. Spin a top on a board. Gently tilt the board in different directions. What happens to the axis of the top? What happens to its precession? Does it drift more or less than on a flat surface?

2. Hold a piece of string tightly between your hands. Touch the side of the spinning top with the string. What happens to the drift of the top? What happens to the top when you touch the string to the other side?

3. Put a small piece of clay or a dab of rubber cement on one side of your top. The weight of the top is now uneven. Set the top spinning. What happens to its precession? Does it start sooner or later than when there is no weight?

4. Freeze some water in a large pan to make a sheet of ice. Make a small hole in the ice to hold the point of the top. Set it spinning in the hole. Does the top spin longer than on other hard surfaces? Does it take longer for precession to appear? Is friction more or less on an icy surface?

6  GYROSCOPES

A gyroscope top is a top in a frame. You can hold it by its frame without touching the spinning flywheel and slowing it down. You can feel the way the top fights you when you move it around in the air. The faster a gyroscope spins and the heavier the flywheel, the harder it is to change the direction of the gyroscope's axis.

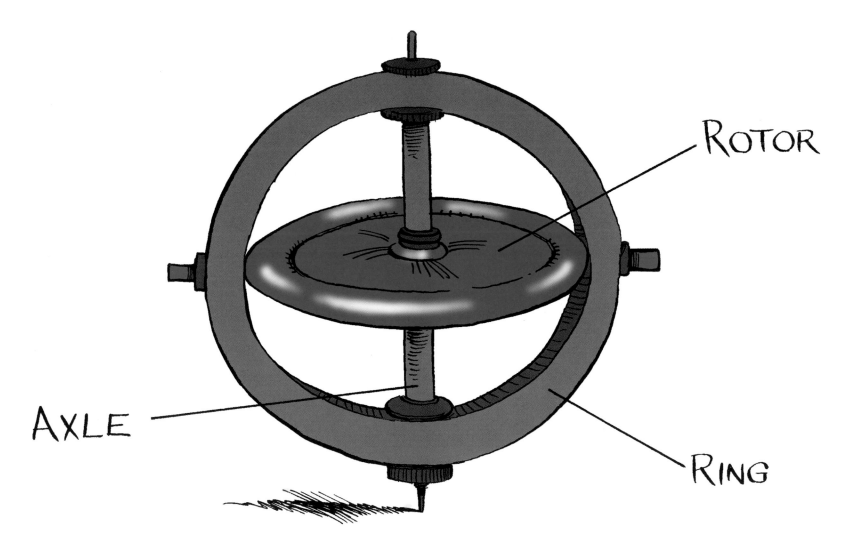

Your two-wheel bicycle is the best example of a gyroscope at work. When you aren't moving, the bike cannot balance on its tires. Everything changes when the wheels are spinning. The wheel axis is in a horizontal direction, parallel to the ground. The wheels themselves are at right angles to the axis and the ground. When a gyroscope is spinning, it resists a change in the direction of the axis. So when the wheels on your bike are moving, there is a force keeping you in an upright position. In fact, the faster you go, the easier it is to stay balanced on two wheels.

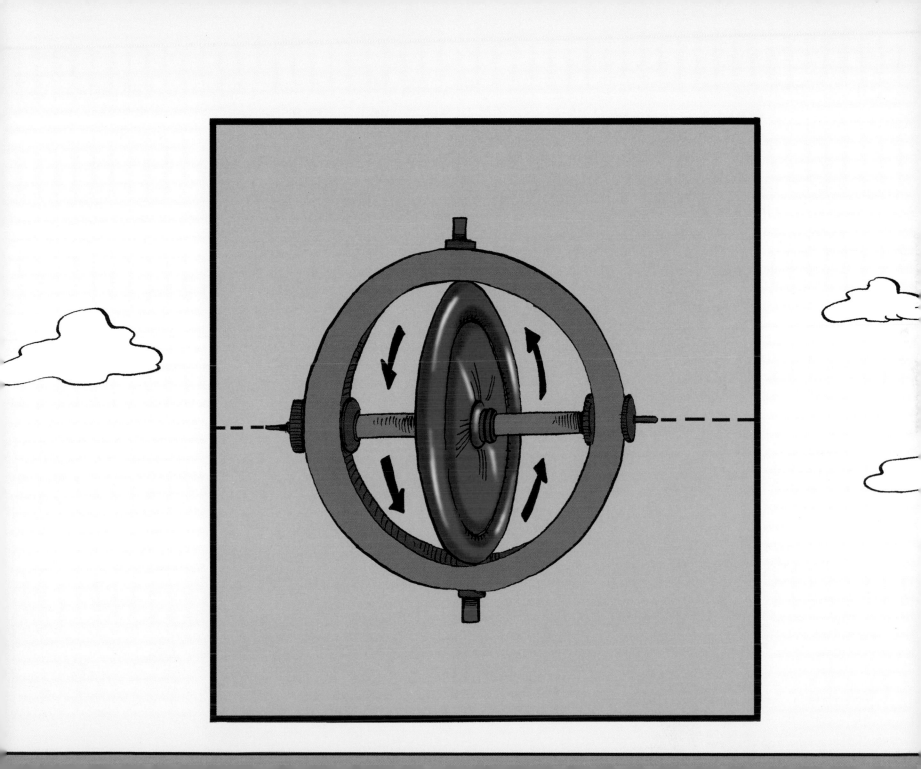

A gyroscope can be hung between two points of attachment called gimbals. The gimbals allow the gyroscope to remain in its original position even if the gimbals are attached to something that changes direction, like a ship or an airplane. Gyroscopes are used in airplanes to create an artificial horizon. This way the pilot knows how far the wings are tilting when making a turn.

NO MATTER WHICH WAY THE PLANE TILTS, THIS AXLE IS ALWAYS PARALLEL TO THE HORIZON.

Navigational systems use two gyroscopes with the axles at right angles to each other. They are set on a platform inside a set of gimbals. No matter which way the vessel moves, sensors can tell exactly where it is heading and how its motion is changing in all three directions. These systems are used in planes and rocket ships to keep them on course.

IGOR, THE PLANE IS UPSIDE DOWN!